Leaving My Homeland
After the Journey

Hoping for a Home After Myanmar

CRABTREE
PUBLISHING COMPANY
WWW.CRABTREEBOOKS.COM

Ellen Rodger

CRABTREE
PUBLISHING COMPANY
WWW.CRABTREEBOOKS.COM

Author: Ellen Rodger

Editors: Sarah Eason, Harriet McGregor, and Janine Deschenes

Proofreader and indexer: Wendy Scavuzzo

Editorial director: Kathy Middleton

Design: Paul Myerscough and Jessica Moon

Cover design: Samara Parent

Photo research: Rachel Blount

Production coordinator and
Prepress technician: Ken Wright

Print coordinator: Katherine Berti

Consultants: Hawa Sabriye and HaEun Kim, Centre for Refugee Studies, York University

Produced for Crabtree Publishing Company by Calcium Creative

Publisher's Note: The story presented in this book is a fictional account based on extensive research of real-life accounts by refugees, with the aim of reflecting the true experience of refugee children and their families.

Photo Credits:
t=Top, c=Center, b=Bottom, l= Left, r=Right

Inside: Jessica Moon: pp. 6t, 29b; Shutterstock: Aisyaqilumaranas: p. 13; Sk Hasan Ali: pp. 9b, 9c; Asantosg: p. 4tl; Ashadhodhomei: p. 18c; Drogatnev: p. 24b; Suphapong Eiamvorasombat: p. 7; Great Vector Elements: p. 10t; Elenabsl: p. 26t; Iconic Bestiary: pp. 18t, 19br; Ideyweb: p. 19tr; Isovector: p. 18b; Jemastock: p. 11c; Hafiz Johari: p. 14t; Kamarulzamanganu: p. 15c; Helga Khorimarko: pp. 10cl, 16t, 26b; TK Kurikawa: p. 21t; Laboo Studio: pp. 4b, 27b; Lano Lan: p. 12t; LineTale: p. 17b; MicroOn: p. 3; Amrul Azuar Mokhtar: p. 25t; Mspoint: p. 28t; MSSA: pp. 9t, 14b; Aizuddin Saad: p. 29t; Sam's Studio: pp. 16-17c; Djohan Shahrin: p. 15t; Sldesign: p. 4tr; Stmoo: p. 21c; Gaie Uchel: pp. 10c, 12b, 20; Chanwit Whanset: p. 6b; What's My Name: p. 23t; UNHCR: © UNHCR/Roger Arnold: pp. 16-17b, 22; © UNHCR/Mimi Zarina Azmin: pp. 19bl, 26c; © UNHCR/Babar Baloch: p. 11t; © UNHCR/Tarmizy Harva: p. 27t; © UNHCR/Sarah Hoibak: p. 28b; © UNHCR/Andrew McConnell: p. 24c; © UNHCR/Kirsty McFadden: p. 19tl; © UNHCR/Kitty McKinsey: p. 23; © UNHCR/Keane Shum: p. 17t.

Cover: Shutterstock: Djohan Shahrin.

Library and Archives Canada Cataloguing in Publication

Rodger, Ellen, author
    Hoping for a home after Myanmar / Ellen Rodger.

(Leaving my homeland : after the journey)
Includes index.
Issued in print and electronic formats.
ISBN 978-0-7787-4974-5 (hardcover).--
ISBN 978-0-7787-4987-5 (softcover).--ISBN 978-1-4271-2123-3 (HTML)

    1. Refugees--Burma--Juvenile literature. 2. Refugees--United States--Juvenile literature. 3. Refugee children--Burma--Juvenile literature. 4. Refugee children--United States--Juvenile literature. 5. Refugees--Social conditions--Juvenile literature. 6. Refugees--United States--Social conditions--Juvenile literature. 7. Burma--Social conditions--Juvenile literature. 8. Boat people--Burma--Juvenile literature. 9. Boat people--United States--Juvenile literature.
    I. Title.

HV640.5.B93R653 2018   j305.9'0691409591073   C2018-903010-0
                                       C2018-903011-9

Library of Congress Cataloging-in-Publication Data

Names: Rodger, Ellen, author.
Title: Hoping for a home after Myanmar / Ellen Rodger.
Description: New York : Crabtree Publishing, [2019] |
  Series: Leaving my homeland: after the journey | Includes index.
Identifiers: LCCN 2018029234 (print) | LCCN 2018032289 (ebook) |
  ISBN 9781427121233 (Electronic) |
  ISBN 9780778749745 (hardcover) |
  ISBN 9780778749875 (pbk.)
Subjects: LCSH: Refugees--Burma--Juvenile literature. | Refugees--
  Malaysia--Juvenile literature. | Refugee children--Malaysia--Juvenile
  literature. | Burmese--Malaysia--Juvenile literature.
Classification: LCC HV640.5.B93 (ebook) |
  LCC HV640.5.B93 R639 2019 (print) | DDC 305.23089/914--dc23
LC record available at https://lccn.loc.gov/2018029234

Crabtree Publishing Company
www.crabtreebooks.com   1-800-387-7650

Printed in the U.S.A./092018/CG20180719

Published in Canada
Crabtree Publishing
616 Welland Ave.
St. Catharines, Ontario
L2M 5V6

Published in the United States
Crabtree Publishing
PMB 59051
350 Fifth Avenue, 59th Floor
New York, New York 10118

Published in the United Kingdom
Crabtree Publishing
Maritime House
Basin Road North, Hove
BN41 1WR

Published in Australia
Crabtree Publishing
3 Charles Street
Coburg North
VIC, 3058

What Is in This Book?

Syed's Story: Myanmar to Malaysia

Hello! I am Syed. I live in Malaysia. I used to live in Sittwe, Rakhine State, in Myanmar, my homeland. Many of my uncles, aunts, and cousins lived there, too. It is where my mother is buried. She died when I was 10 years old. Now, my family has fled Myanmar.

Myanmar's flag

Malaysia's flag is called the Stripes of Glory.

We are Rohingya. We had to leave so we could live. In Myanmar, people hate us because we are **Muslim**. They think we do not belong there. The army and police attack us and kill us.

These two Rohingya children live in Malaysia. They go to a school for orphans (children without parents).

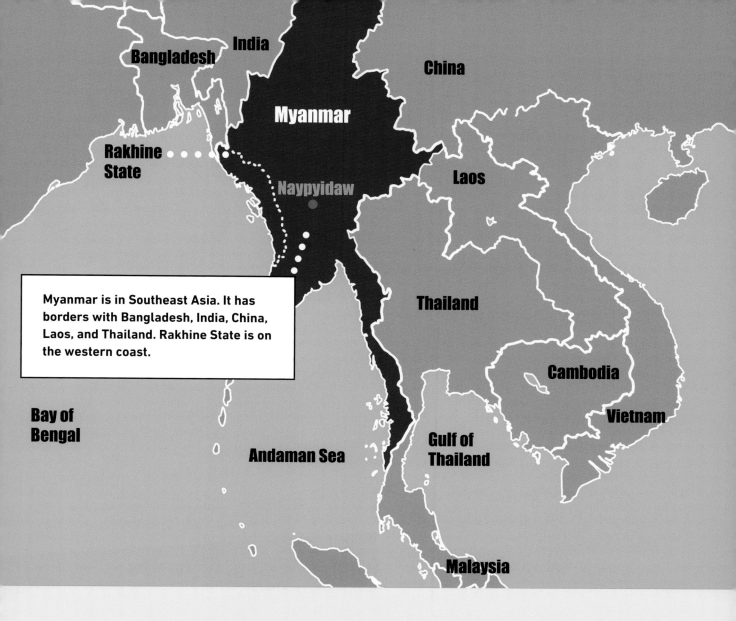

Bangladesh

India

China

Myanmar

Rakhine State

Naypyidaw

Laos

Thailand

Cambodia

Vietnam

Bay of Bengal

Andaman Sea

Gulf of Thailand

Malaysia

Myanmar is in Southeast Asia. It has borders with Bangladesh, India, China, Laos, and Thailand. Rakhine State is on the western coast.

Now I live with my brother Nazir in Malaysia. My baba (father) first paid a **smuggler** to take Nazir to Malaysia. Later, my father paid a lot of money so we too could make the voyage. But it was a terrible journey. My father died. I landed in Indonesia. I stayed in a **refugee** camp for a while. Nazir saved money to pay more smugglers to take me to Malaysia. I was 11 years old.

UN Rights of the Child

A child's family has the **responsibility** to help ensure their **rights** are protected and to help them learn to exercise their rights. Think about these rights as you read this book.

My Homeland, Myanmar

Myanmar is the second-largest country in Southeast Asia. It is covered with tropical forests. The forests are home to animals such as tigers, pythons, and Asian elephants.

Myanmar has a population of 51.5 million people. About 70 percent of these people live in the countryside. People from more than 135 different **ethnic groups** live in Myanmar. The Rohingya people are an ethnic group. They have lived in Myanmar for centuries. They mostly live in the western state of Rakhine.

Myanmar used to be called Burma. Its official name was changed in 1989.

These temples are in Rakhine State. Buddhists (people who follow the Buddhist religion) in Myanmar worship at them.

Hundreds of Rohingya villages in Rakhine State have been destroyed by Myanmar's army.

The Rohingya are Muslims and follow the religion of Islam. Most people in Myanmar follow the religion of Buddhism. The government of Myanmar does not believe that the Rohingya belong in the country. Since 1982, it has not allowed the Rohingya people **citizenship**.

There is a lot of violence in Rakhine State. The Rohingya are persecuted. This means they are treated with extreme cruelty. They are not allowed their rights. Many have been attacked and killed by the army and other people. Hundreds of thousands of Rohingya have fled Myanmar. They are refugees.

Syed's Story: Leaving My Homeland

When we left Sittwe, I felt I would never see my home again. Baba said we could no longer stay. Everyone who could leave was going. No one knew if they would live to see another day.

Baba paid smugglers to take us to Malaysia. He had to borrow the money from our relatives. The smuggler's boat took us out at night. There were so many people on the boat. We hardly had any room. After about a week, people became sick. Some of them died. We were supposed to go to Malaysia. But a navy ship towed us away from land, then took our engine. We had no power then, and we drifted under the hot sun.

Bangladesh

Myanmar

Sittwe, Rakhine State

Thailand

Andaman Sea

Malaysia

Sumatra

The journey across the sea to Malaysia is very dangerous. Storms sometimes destroy the boats that people travel in.

The smugglers did not care if we lived or died. Baba did not have enough food or water. He became weak and sick. Then, he died. I wanted to take our bag of belongings from Baba's body, but a smuggler saw it and stole it.

I do not like to talk or think about Baba's death. There was no burial. Only me and a few others said prayers. I was alone. I thought I would die, too. After more than a month, the boat landed in Sumatra, Indonesia. There, we were put in camps but I did not stay there long. A man with a phone let me contact my brother Nazir. He arranged for men to smuggle me to him in Malaysia.

Story in Numbers

In 2015, an estimated

25,000

Rohingya left Myanmar in boats. In 2017,

671,000

Rohingya left Myanmar, and traveled to Bangladesh.

These Rohingya refugees have traveled to Bangladesh. They are waiting at the border between Myanmar and Bangladesh.

After weeks of walking, these refugees must cross a river to Bangladesh. There, they will live in refugee camps.

A New Life

The Rohingya people have been fleeing Myanmar for decades. Since 2017, large-scale attacks on Rohingyas have created a **crisis**. Thousands have left to escape the violence. Some countries have given the Rohingya asylum. Asylum means safety or protection from harm.

There are almost no schools open to Rohingya children in Malaysia. This religious school in Kuala Lumpur, Malaysia, does accept Rohingya.

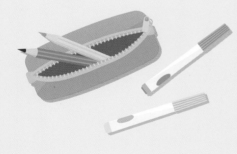

If someone is given asylum by a country, it usually means they can stay there for a while. But it does not always mean the country helps support them with food or money. Asylum seekers can apply for **refugee status**. The **United Nations High Commissioner for Refugees (UNHCR)** is an international organization that registers refugees. Once a refugee has refugee status, they have legal rights. They cannot be sent back to their homeland by force.

In Malaysia, Rohingya men often live together to share costs. It is difficult for them to make money because the law there says they are not allowed to work.

But not all countries allow refugees their rights. Many countries do not have written rules or ways of dealing with refugees. If an asylum seeker lands in one of these countries, they cannot be sure they can stay, work legally, or go to school. In Malaysia, everyday life for Rohingya asylum seekers and refugees is very difficult. People can only work illegally and children usually cannot go to school.

Story in Numbers

Rohingya refugees in nearby countries:
Bangladesh: 1 million
Pakistan: 350,000
Saudi Arabia: 200,000
Malaysia: 150,000
India: 40,000
United Arab Emirates (UAE): 10,000
Thailand: 5,000
Indonesia: 1,000

Syed's Story: Arriving in Malaysia

When I first came here to Malaysia, I knew nothing. I could not speak English or the local language, Malay. Nazir became like a father to me. He told me what to do, where to go, and even what to eat. Nazir said I must not trust anyone. He said we do not know who will do us harm. I must not cause any trouble. If I get into trouble, I will be put in jail or maybe even kicked out of the country.

In Malaysia, the Rohingya must get used to a new **culture** with different foods, such as those sold at this Malaysian market.

Rohingya children spend long days at work with their parents, while they try to earn money to support them.

Nazir works in construction. He helped me get a job, too. I move bags of concrete, clean up, and make tea for the workers. I work for whatever money they give me.

Nazir and I live with our cousins Saddiq and Ibrahim. They are like brothers to us. Saddiq has a cell phone. Every week, we use instant messenger to call or text our uncles. Sometimes, we can see them on video chat. We owe a lot of money to my Gera (Uncle) Abdul. But he said we do not have to pay back the **loan** because it was made to my father. When we can afford to, we send him money anyway. It is our duty. We know he has many people to support.

Construction is one area of work in which refugees can work illegally.

As-Salaam-Alaikum (Peace be with you) Gera Abdul,
Thank you for your prayers. We are well and working. I am now a tea boy for the builders. I buy tea at the market nearby. There are many tea-makers there. I got a deal with one. I pay less because I always come to him. I also practice my Malay with him. He does not seem happy, but he calls me a smart boy.
Bye for now,
Syed

13

A New Home

The Rohingya people have had no **security** for the last 50 years. Nearly 1 million have left Myanmar since the late 1970s. Some go by boat to Malaysia, Thailand, or Indonesia. Others go to Saudi Arabia, Pakistan, India, and the UAE. The **United Nations (UN)** also believes that 120,000 Rohingya have left their homes but are still in Myanmar. They are **internally displaced persons (IDPs)**.

Hundreds of thousands of Rohingya live in Bangladesh in refugee camps near the border. Most are unregistered. The Bangladeshi military run the camps. They control who enters and leaves the camps. Children go to school in the camps. The Bangladeshi government wants to send the Rohingya back to Myanmar.

These Bangladeshi soldiers are keeping order in a Rohingya refugee camp.

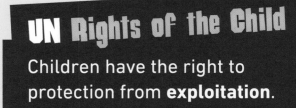

UN Rights of the Child

Children have the right to protection from **exploitation**.

In the Bangladesh camps, refugees are given food aid. This Rohingya boy is carrying a bag of rice.

Refugee camps in Bangladesh are overcrowded. Some homes are made of scrap wood, metal, and plastic coverings.

In Malaysia, the government agreed to accept refugees. But there are no camps there. To support themselves, refugees work illegally in jobs that are often unsafe and not well paid.

Rohingya refugees in Malaysia have no legal rights. They are often exploited. They may be put in detention. Detention is like jail. Refugees can be held in detention for weeks or years. Many Rohingya have died from disease while in detention.

Syed's Story: My New Home

The city where we live is called Kuala Lumpur. It is a big city—bigger than any city I have ever seen before. Nazir says we are lucky because there is work close to us. Our house is small. It has one room where we all sleep on the floor. There are nine of us Rohingya here, including my cousins, a family with two children, and another man. That man, Kamal, has lived here for 20 years.

Kuala Lumpur has a population of 1.8 million people. They are spread out over several districts.

One of the children goes to a community school in our neighborhood. It is run by a charity. It teaches math and English. If I did not need to work, I would go to the school, too. I would like to learn and improve my math. In Malaysia, some people are good, but there are others you cannot trust. They attack Rohingya. However, it is still better here than back home—they may not like us here, but they do not hate us enough to kill us.

Rohingya refugees live all over Southeast Asia and the **Middle East**. Cell phones and video calling apps help people keep in contact with family.

*We have not heard from our family in Myanmar for two weeks. Kamal said he heard there is more trouble there. Whole villages have been destroyed. People are fleeing to Bangladesh. But they are being killed as they leave. He heard this at the place where he goes to send money home. I think I believe him. But Nazir said we should ask others at the **mosque**.*

Only 30 percent of Rohingya children go to school in Malaysia. This student is studying at the Refugee Learning Center in Kuala Lumpur.

Story in Numbers

Refugees make about

20 ringgit ($5)

a day for shifts that last as long as 12 hours.

A New Mosque

There are few organizations that help Rohingya refugees in Malaysia. When refugees arrive, they rely on friends and family already in the country. These people help refugees find jobs and a place to live.

Mosques are important community meeting places, as well as places of prayer. Refugees can stay in them for a short time, until they find jobs and places to live. Rohingya refugees also set up *suraus*. These are smaller places where people pray. Refugees meet with people from their own culture there.

Mosques such as this one in Kuala Lumpur help Rohingya connect and support one another.

UN Rights of the Child

Children have the right to a good quality education and should be encouraged to go to school to the highest level they can attain.

This Rohingya Education Center in Kuala Lumpur is run with the support of the UNHCR. The teacher is Malaysian. Around 120 children attend the school.

Mosques and some churches operate schools for refugee children. The schools provide basic education in English, Malay, and math. Some schools use **volunteer** teachers. These teachers are not always available to teach. Rohingya children almost never attend secondary school. They can only do so if their parents have enough money to pay for private schools. Many go to religious schools run by mosques. These provide religious education.

These children are enjoying sports day at a school for Rohingya in Kuala Lumpur. Rohingya refugee children have few chances to play and have fun.

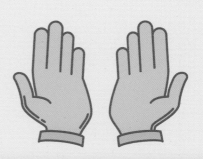

Syed's Story: A New Way of Learning

*I do not go to school. All my learning is done at my work or at home. Last month, our construction site was **raided** by police. They were looking for illegal workers. Luckily, they did not catch us. Nazir and I ran away as fast as we could. If they had caught us, they would have put us in detention.*

Luckily, Saddiq got Nazir another job at a construction site farther away from home. A Malaysian man who is one of our neighbors helped Saddiq buy a motorbike. Now, Saddiq and Nazir can travel to work on it. Saddiq could not buy the motorcycle himself because he is not here legally. The man did not even take a fee for helping us. He said it was his duty to help a brother Muslim.

These Rohingya refugees have been caught by the police for working illegally. But if they do not work, they cannot support themselves and their families.

People gather at outside restaurants in Malaysia. Some restaurants hire Rohingya refugees to work in the kitchens.

We heard news last week that there is more trouble in Rakhine. The army is killing many Rohingya. Nobody can stop it. Four of my uncles have left Myanmar. They are going to the camps in Bangladesh. One of my uncles and his family are missing. It is very bad.

Dear uncles,
I am well, but very worried about all of you. I am praying that you are well. I have some good news. Since the raid last month, Nazir and I have new jobs. We can send you some money! Ibrahim helped me get a job washing dishes in a restaurant. It is a good job and they give me meals to eat. I am learning English from one of the cooks. I already know Malay. In fact, I know it better than Nazir! I will work hard so I can help you.
Bye for now,
Syed

Everything Changes

There are organizations in Malaysia that help Rohingya refugees who do not speak Malay or English. These are run by Rohingya people and supported by community donations. They also help fellow Rohingya register with the UNHCR.

Refugees registered with the UNHCR receive cards that give them some security. The cards allow them to go to the hospital if they have the money to pay. Being registered also gives Rohingya some hope that they could start a new life—but only if a foreign country agrees to accept them.

This Rohingya woman is in a refugee camp. She is holding her refugee card. This proves she has been registered by the UNHCR.

UN Rights of the Child

Children have the right to an identity, or official record, of who they are, and the right to a nationality.

The UNHCR has been helping the Rohingya for decades. Here, they are giving out temporary identity cards.

Many Rohingya refugees do not believe they will be able to return to Myanmar. Right now, it is too dangerous. The Rohingya also do not believe that the Myanmar government will ever accept them or give them back their citizenship rights. Their only hope is to make a new life in Malaysia or to find a new home in another country.

The Rohingya share the same religion as most people in Malaysia—Islam. But even Rohingya people who have lived there 30 years feel they will never be fully accepted. This is true for Rohingya living as refugees in other Muslim countries, too. Rohingya children born in Malaysia have Malaysian birth certificates, but they still cannot become citizens.

Syed's Story: My New Way of Life

Things change here every day. Ibrahim has moved to another city to run a tea shop with his mother's cousin. Kamal has also moved. It is getting harder for Rohingya to come to Malaysia. But our cousin Quyum has just arrived. He lives here now with his wife and children.

The house is busy with four little children and six adults. Nazir and I do not mind. Quyum's wife Najimah looks after us like a sister. Nazir is embarrassed sometimes because she fusses over him. But I like it. We bring her food from the market and she cooks the things I like. She reminds me of my mother.

It took these Rohingya four hours to cross the Naf River on a raft to reach Bangladesh.

Many Rohingya refugees say they do not have plans to return to Myanmar. They do not feel it will ever be safe in their homeland.

*Quyum told us many terrible stories about what is happening in Rakhine. The army is killing people and setting fire to Rohingya homes. Najimah's mother escaped to Bangladesh with her youngest son and his family. They are now in the same camp as my uncles. We have saved money to pay for a **bribe** if ever the police caught us working here. But we must now send that money to our uncles to help them.*

As-Salaam-Alaikum Gera Abdul,
We are so happy that you and your family are safe. Your long journey to Bangladesh must have been so scary. Cousin Quyum and his family have arrived here safely. Quyum is looking for work. If you can tell us where to send money, Nazir will send some today. Please use some of the money to buy a phone, so you can stay in contact. Please tell us how everyone is and who is with you.
Alhamdulillah (Praise God)

Syed's Story: Looking to the Future

A man who comes to the restaurant is a doctor and friend of my boss. He said that if I go to the Rohingya community school and do well, he will pay for me to go to a private school. I cannot believe my luck! Neither can Nazir. He wants to meet with this man to see if he is honest. If I can go to a private school, I can learn so much. Maybe then I can get a better job or go to secondary school.

If refugee children can get an education, they have a chance to make a better life.

UN Rights of the Child

Children have the right to special care and help if they cannot live with their parents.

Some Rohingya children become separated from their families when they flee Myanmar. They hope to be reunited with them at some point in the future.

These Rohingya men in Malaysia are protesting about the treatment of their people in Rakhine State.

Nazir pays a man to send letters to the UNHCR office each month. He asks them to help us be resettled. Sometimes we hear stories about the United States or Canada taking Rohingya refugees. Other times, it is Australia. After many months of waiting, we no longer get excited about these stories. But Nazir thinks we still have to remind the UNHCR office that we exist.

Sometimes, I think about how things would be if my father was still alive. This makes me sad. When Najimah sees this, she asks me to sit with her. She makes me tell her all about my father and my mother and all the other people that I have lost. "If we remember them, they will not be lost to us," she says.

Do Not Forget Our Stories!

Rohingya child refugees often travel alone to refugee camps in Bangladesh. Many have lost their entire families in the violence in Myanmar. The young refugees walk for days. Some are helped by other Rohingya refugees along the way. Rohingya child refugees have also fled to Malaysia, Thailand, and Pakistan.

Child refugees do not have any way to take care of themselves. They must rely on strangers. Very often, child refugees must work long hours for low pay. They do not go to school. This might be because there are no schools for them. Or it might be because they must work to feed themselves instead.

Many Rohingya children begin school late in Malaysia. If given a chance, they can catch up in their learning.

There are many things we can do to help refugees. One important thing is to not forget their stories. Refugees are resilient. This means they can recover from difficult times. Refugees build strong communities. They contribute to their new countries. But many need help to build new lives. All refugees want a home where they can live, work, or go to school in peace.

The Rohingya want the world to know what is happening to them. Maybe then, governments will help stop the violence.

Discussion Prompts

1. Why do some countries not want to help refugees such as the Rohingya?
2. How do refugees such as the Rohingya help improve the communities where they live?
3. What makes child refugees a special group? Do you think you could survive in a foreign land without parents to take care of you?

Glossary

bribe Money paid to someone so that they will act in your favor

citizenship Being legal members of a country and having the rights of that country

crisis An intense time of difficulty

culture The shared beliefs, values, traditions, arts, and ways of life of a group of people

ethnic groups Groups of people who have the same nation, culture, and religion

exploitation To take unfair advantage of someone

internally displaced persons (IDPs) People who are forced from their homes during a conflict but remain in the country

loan Money that is borrowed and paid back later

Middle East Countries in southwestern Asia and northern Africa that stretch from Libya to Afghanistan

mosque A Muslim place of worship

Muslim A follower of Islam

raided Suddenly and unexpectedly entered

refugee A person who flees from his or her own country to another due to unsafe conditions

refugee status To be a refugee in the eyes of the law and be eligible for asylum

responsibility The duty to deal with something

rights Privileges and freedoms protected by law

security Freedom from danger or threat

smuggler A person who moves people or things illegally

United Nations (UN) An international organization of 193 countries that promotes peace between countries and helps refugees

United Nations High Commissioner for Refugees (UNHCR) A program that protects and supports refugees everywhere

unregistered Not officially recorded

volunteer Someone who offers to work for no pay

Learning More

Books

Mara, Wil. *Myanmar* (Enchantment of the World). Children's Press, 2016.

Roberts, Ceri. *Refugees and Migrants* (Children's World). Barron's Educational Series, 2017.

Ruurs, Margriet. *Stepping Stones: A Refugee Family's Journey*. Orca Book Publishers, 2016.

Websites

www.bbc.co.uk/newsround/41242024
Visit this website for detailed information about what is happening in Myanmar today.

www.unhcr.org/ibelong/what-does-it-mean-to-be-stateless
The Rohingya people are stateless. Watch this short video about what it means to be stateless.

www.unicef.org/rightsite/files/uncrcchilldfriendlylanguage.pdf
Read about the United Nations Convention on the Rights of the Child.

Film

Unfairy Tales
A series of three animated movies produced by UNICEF that tell the stories of refugee children Malak, Ivine, and Mustafa. Suitable for children aged eight and up.

Index

About the Author

Ellen Rodger is a descendant of refugees who fled persecution and famine. She has written and edited many books for children and adults on subjects as varied as potatoes, how government works, social justice, war, soccer, and lice and fleas.